THE MINISTER'S CAT

THE
MINISTER'S CAT

COMPILED BY
Hamish Whyte

ILLUSTRATED BY
Barbara Robertson

ABERDEEN UNIVERSITY PRESS
1991

First published 1991
Aberdeen University Press

A catalogue record for this book is available from
the British Library.

ISBN 0 08 041208 4

Design by Mark Blackadder
Typeset by Hewer Text Composition Services,
Edinburgh
Printed by Martin's of Berwick Ltd

Acknowledgements

Grateful acknowledgement is made to the Scottish National Dictionary Association for permission to include extracts from *The Concise Scots Dictionary* (AUP, 1985) and for allowing the dictionary to be used in this way. I should like to thank all those who helped the game along with information and suggestions: Simon Berry, Anne Escott, Joe Fisher, Janice Galloway, Kevin McCarra, Adam McNaughtan, Graeme and Margaret Whyte. Special thanks to Babs Robertson for her drawings which really make the book. And thanks, as ever, to Winifred for her encouragement and her critical eye.

INTRODUCTION

'The Minister's Cat' is familiar to most Scots. It is an alphabet game, played by any number: in each round each player has to think of an epithet for the cat beginning with the same letter of the alphabet. 'The minister's cat is a . . . cat.' The game works through A to Z and a player who fails to come up with an appropriate adjective is out. It is not really a competitive game in the sense of there being a winner; rather, players try to outdo each other in thinking of extravagant terms for the cat. It's played for fun.

In my experience it is a family game. I associate it with my granny. The Minister's Cat joined other games such as hunt-the-thimble (or Grandpa's half-crown) at the New Year get-together of family and friends.

It is described thus in Alice Bertha Gomme's monumental *The Traditional Games of England, Scotland, and Ireland* (vol. I, 1894): 'The first player begins by saying, "The minister's cat is an ambitious cat," the next player "an artful cat," and so on, until they have all named an adjective beginning with A. The next time of going round the adjectives must begin with B, the next time C, and so on, until the whole of the alphabet has been gone through.'

Interestingly, the informants named by Alice Gomme as supplying her with the details of the game were from the Forest of Dean, Gloucestershire, and Anderby in Lincolnshire. Obviously, the game is, or was, played in England. I have always regarded it as peculiarly Scottish, probably because minister is the usual term applied to Scottish clergymen. However, in England, although not used of Anglican clergymen, minister is, as the *Shorter Oxford English Dictionary* puts it, 'chiefly associated with Low Church views; but still usual in non-episcopal communions.' But then, why a minister (or vicar, parson or priest) in the first place? Why not the doctor's cat, the baker's cat or the candlestick maker's? Perhaps the cat was generally felt to be a fit companion to a man of the cloth: an independent kind of pet fit for a bachelor (as many ministers are), a pet, at least in England, suitably non-conformist? (There is, by the way, a minister's dog: the name of a Tweed salmon fly, made originally from the yellow hairs of the minister of Sprouston's dog in 1915.)

A number of clerical ailurophiles are listed in Christobel Aberconway's *Dictionary of Cat Lovers* (Michael Joseph, 1949): John Jortin D.D., Pope Leo XII, Cardinal Richelieu, Cardinal Wolsey, the Rev. James Woodforde. On this evidence it would seem that Roman Catholic prelates were more potty about pussies than other clergy. Pope Gregory the Great is said to have even made his cat a cardinal! (It is perhaps strange that an animal we tend to link historically with witches should be associated with their traditional persecutors.) But there are even earlier associations with churchmen. The *Book of Lismore* tells the story of three young Irish clerics who went to sea on a pilgrimage with very little provision, but not forgetting their cat which caught fish for them. And the first literary reference in the British Isles to the domestic cat is to be found in a ninth century Irish poem, 'Pangur Ban', about a scholar and his clever cat.

Coming back to Scottish ministers, I have been unable to discover any ministers of the past with cats. There must have been: a mouser would be a must in the manse. I do know that the minister of the church where I grew up had a cat: Mr Towart regularly used Scrap's exploits to point up morals in his children's talks (there was an earlier, more Biblically named cat, Peter, as well). And a Lenzie minister is currently using the game of The Minister's Cat in a similar way.

Whether Scottish or English, the game is certainly a firm favourite in Scotland and what more natural way to play it than by using Scots words. (I am told that the Scots Language Society used to play the game this way at meetings, calling it, predictably, 'The Meenister's Baudrons'.) The words chosen here as examples, illustrated with Barbara Robertson's lovely funny drawings, range from ordinary Scots words like clarty to the more unusual such as veeand. There are old, sometimes obsolete, words, words in contemporary use, words from different parts of the country (the minister's cat is a synthetic cat?). They and their definitions are all taken from *The Concise Scots Dictionary* and a selection of other options (with meanings) are included.

There is also, as is usual, a little cheating.

Scots is such an expressive language for this kind of game (and it often seems, as Barbara Robertson remarked in the course of putting the book together, that all the really fascinating words usually mean 'dirty'). If this compilation has any serious aim it is just to encourage some interest in Scots and not, I hope, to add another tourist bookie to the 'isn't Scots a funny language' pile, though there is always the danger of that. I am no expert on Scots, merely getting to know it – dictionary-trawling for interesting words, remembering words from my childhood and words from reading. Everybody will have their own words and their own style of playing the game. This is only one way of looking at the minister's cat.

The minister's cat is an ALMICHTY cat

almichty &c *15-*, **a'michty** *20-* [alˈmɪxtɪ, ɑˈmɪxtɪ] *adj, also* **almichtine &c** *16*; **almichting &c** *16* = almighty *15-*.
n = Almighty *16-*.

ADVOCATE (barrister)
AFLOCHT (agitated)
AJEE (ajar, off the straight)
ALAGRUOUS
(grim, woebegone)
ALLENARLY (single, only)

The
minister's cat
is a BREENGIN cat.

---

breenge &c *19-*; **brainge &c** [brindʒ; *Fif WC,
SW* brendʒ] *v* **1** *vi* rush forward recklessly or
carelessly; plunge; make a violent effort *la18-*.
2 *vt* drive with a rush; batter, bang *la19-, now
Abd Ags.*
n a violent or clumsy rush, a dash, a plunge
la18-.
breengin &c wilful, pushing, sharp-tongued;
bustling *19-, now local.*

BOGSHAIVELT
(knocked out of shape)
BONNY (pretty)
BRAID (broad)
BLERIT (debauched-looking)
BUCKSTURDIE (obstinate)

The minister's cat is a CLARTY cat

clart¹ &c; clort &c *la19-*, **klurt** *Sh Ork* [klart, klort, klert, klɛrt; *Sh Ork* klʌrt] *n* **1** mud, mire *la19-*. **2** a lump or clot of something unpleasant *19-*. **3** a big, dirty, untidy person *la19-*, *local*.
v **1** *vt* besmear, dirty *19-*. **2** *vi* act in a slovenly, dirty way; work with dirty or sticky substances *20-*, *local*.
∼y 1 dirty, muddy; sticky *la16-*. **2** *of a painting etc* daubed, smudgy *20-*, *Sh Bnf Abd*. [*cf* eME *biclarten* defile]

CADGY (friendly, cheerful)
CAMSTAIRY (quarrelsome)
CANTY (cheerful)
CORRIE-FISTED
(left-handed)
CREESHIE (greasy, fat, dirty)

The minister's cat is a DISJASKIT cat.

disjaskit &c [dɪsˈdʒaskɪt; *Rox also* -ˈdʒeskɪt] *adj*
1 dejected, downcast, depressed *19-*, *local*. **2**
dilapidated, neglected, untidy *18-*, *local*. **3**
exhausted, worn out; weary-looking *19-*, *local*.
[see SND]

DEID (dead)
DOITERED
(confused, as in old age)
DOUR (grim)
DOWIE (dull, weak)
DROUTHY (thirsty)

The
minister's cat is
an EASY OSY cat.

---

easy &c *la16-,* **esy &c** *15-17,* **aisy &c** *16-e20*
adj **1** = easy *15-.* **2** *followed by the gerund (where
Eng would have infin) 19-:* '*It's easy speakin.*'
easy osy &c *adj, of persons* easy-going, inclined
to be lazy; *of things* involving the minimum of
effort *19-.* *n* an easy-going or lazy person *la19-,*
now Bwk.

EIDENT (diligent)
ELDRITCH (weird, unearthly)
EMBRO (Edinburgh)
ESSART (stubborn)
EVILL-AVISIT
(disposed to wrong-doing)

The minister's cat is a FUSHIONLESS cat.

fushion &c *la19-*, **fusioun &c** *la15-17*, **foisoun &c** *la14-18*; **fusoun &c** *la14-15*, **fusion &c** *la14-e20*, **fooshion &c** *e20* ['fuʒən, 'fuʃən, 'fʌʃən; *C, S also* 'føʃən &c] *n* **1** = foison, plenty etc *la14-16*. **2** the nourishing or sustaining element in food or drink *17-*, *now NE Per*. **3** physical strength, energy; bodily sensation, power of feeling *18-*, *now NE*. **4** mental or spiritual force or energy; strength of character, power *18-*, *now NE*.

~less 1 *of plants etc* without sap or pith, dried, withered *19-*, *now local Sh-Arg*. **2** *of food* lacking in nourishment, tasteless, insipid *19-*, *local Sh-C*. **3** *of actions, speech, writing etc* without substance, dull, uninspired *19-*, *now Abd C*. **4** *of persons* (1) physically weak, without energy *18-*; (2) numb, without feeling *la18-*, *NE*. **5** *of things* without strength or durability; weak from decay *19-*. **6** *of persons etc, and their moral or mental qualities* spiritless, faint-hearted, lacking vigour or ability *19-*.

FAUSE (false)
FEART (afraid)
FILSH (weak, faint)
FLISKIE (restless, flighty)
FOOSTY (musty, mouldy)

The minister's cat is a GLEG cat.

gleg &c *adj* **1** *chf of persons* (1) quick, keen in perception, *freq* ~ **of** *or* **in sight, hearing, eye** *etc*, *15-*; (2) quick of movement; nimble, adroit *18-*, *local*; (3) keen, smart, alert, quick-witted, *freq* ~ **in, of** *or* **at the uptak** *la18-*; (4) lively, sprightly; merry *19-*, *now Sh NE Per*. **2** *of the senses, esp the sight* sharp, keen *18-*, *now local Ags-Rox*. **3** *of cutting implements* sharp-pointed, keen-edged *18-*, *now Per WC Ayr*. **4** *of mechanisms* smooth-working, quick-acting *la18-*, *now local Ags-Rox*.

GAMPHERD
(bespangled, adorned)
GASH (smartly dressed)
GAWSIE (plump, handsome)
GIRNIE (ill-tempered)
GLAIKIT (stupid, foolish)

The minister's cat is a HEEPOCH-ONDREOCH cat.

---

heepochondreoch [ˈhipɪkonˈdriəx] *adj* listless, melancholy *20-, Abd Kinr.* [f Eng *hypochondriac*, w different stress accentuation; see also HYPOCHONDERIES]

HALLACH (crazy, hare-brained)
HAPPITY (lame)
HEICH (tall, high)
HIELAND (Highland)
HYTE (mad, enraged)

The
minister's cat
is an IN-KNEED cat.

---

in-kneed, in-kne'd *adj* knock-kneed *17-, now Ork N Rox.*

IDLESET (idle)
ILL-HAUDEN (oppressed)
INFAME (infamous)
IVIL (evil)

The minister's cat is a JOCO cat.

joco &c [dʒəˈko] *adj* jovial, merry, cheerful, pleased with oneself *la19-, Gen except Sh Ork*. [reduced f Eng *jocose*]

JAFFLED (tired, worn out)
JAGGIE (prickly)
JIMP (small, neat, scanty)
JONICK (genuine, honest)
JOUKING (ducking, dodging)

The minister's cat is a KIRKIE cat.

kirk &c *n* **1** = church *la14-, in place-names la12-* (see DOST). **2** (1) *esp* before the Reformation, applied to the Roman Catholic Church, in Scotland and beyond *16-e17*; (2) after the Reformation, applied to the reformed church in Scotland both when episcopalian and when presbyterian in organization; since *la17* largely replaced by CHURCH in most formal contexts, but reappearing in recent years, *usu* as **the K~**, in all contexts except the official title *Church of Scotland* (CHURCH) *la16-*; see also ~ *session*, PRESBYTERY, SYNOD, *general assembly* (GENERAL), FREE, *Reformed Presbyterian Church* (REFORM), RELIEF, *seceder* (SECEDE), UNITED. **3** the ruling body or *kirk-session* of a local church *la16-e17*. **4** the *General Assembly* (GENERAL) of the *Church of Scotland* (CHURCH) *la16-e17*.

vt, chf in passive = be churched, *orig chf* of the first church attendance after a birth or marriage, *latterly* (*la19-*) also after a funeral or *eg* on the appointment of a civic or academic body *15-*.

~ie &c enthusiastically devoted to church affairs *20-, local*.

KELVINSIDE
(Glasgow West End affected)
KENSPECKLE (conspicuous, familiar)
KITTLIE (susceptible to tickling)
KNACKIE (skilful, smart)

The
minister's cat
is a LALLAN cat.

lallan *la18-*; **laland &c** ['lalǝn] *n* **1** *latterly in pl*
= LAWLAND *n* 2, *la16-e19*. **2** *now chf in pl* (1)
= SCOTS (*n* 1) *la18-*; (2) *specif* since about 1940,
the variety of literary SCOTS (*n* 1) used by writ-
ers of the Scottish Renaissance movement.
adj **1** = LAWLAND *adj, 18-, now local Kcdn-Ayr.* **2**
using the speech of the *Lowlands* (LAWLAND) of
Scotland, SCOTS-speaking as opposed to GAELIC-
or English-speaking *la18-*.

LAITHLY (loathsome)
LEAL (faithful)
LEELIKE (lying, fictional)
LOURDIE (heavy, sluggish)
LOWPAN (leaping, bounding)

The
minister's cat
is a MAUKIT cat.

mauk &c *18-*, **mauch &c** *e16, 19-* [mɑk; *nEC* mɑx] *n* a maggot *16-*, *Gen except NE.*
~**ie &c** **1** maggoty *la18-, now Fif.* **2** filthy *19-, now Inv Edb.* ~**ie fly** = ~ *flee, 20-, S.* **maukit, maucht** *adj* **1** *esp of sheep* infested with maggots *19-, Cai C, S.* **2** putrid; filthy *la20-, WC.* **3** exhausted, played out *20-, S.*

MAISTERFU
(overbearing, powerful)
MARDLE (clumsy, lazy)
MINGIN (smelly)
MIRACULOUS (very drunk)
MUCKLE (big, great)

The
minister's cat
is a NURRING cat.

---

nurr; njirr *la19-, Sh-Cai* [n(j)ʌr; *Sh Ork* njɪr] *vi* **1** growl like an angry dog, snarl like a cat *19-, now Sh Cai.* **2** *of a cat* purr *19-, chf Sh.*
n the growl or snarl of an angry dog *19-, now Sh Rox.*
~**ing &c** growling, snarling; fault-finding *19-, now Sh Cai.* [imit; *cf* NARR and Norw *knurre,* Du *knorren* (*v*) growl, OE *gnyrran* creak]

NAPPY (slightly intoxicated)
NATTERIE (peevish)
NEBBIE (nippy, cheeky)
NESTIE (nasty)
NIRLIE (stunted)

The minister's cat is an ORRA cat.

orra *17-*; **ora** *18-e20*, **orray &c** *la16-e19*, **orrow** *la18-19* ['ɔrə; *C also* *'ɔrɪ] *adj* **1** (1) *of persons or things* spare, unoccupied; unemployed *la16-*, *now Sh-Per*. (2) *specif of women* unattached (either in marriage or as a servant) *la16-17, C.* (3) *specif of one of a pair* without a partner; unmatched, odd *19-*, *Sh-Ags.* **2** spare, extra, odd, superfluous *18-*, *now NE nEC, WC.* **3** (1) occasional, coming at irregular or infrequent intervals, appearing here and there *la18-*, *local NE-S.* (2) *specif* (a) *of a job* casual, odd, unskilled *19-*; (b) *of a person or animal* doing casual or unskilled work *la19-*. **4** miscellaneous, nondescript *19-*, *now NE Ags Per.* **5** strange, uncommon, abnormal *la19-*, *now EC.* **6** *of persons or things* worthless, shabby, disreputable *19-*, *NE Ags Per.*

OFFEECIOUS (officious)
OGERTFU (fastidious)
ONFOWLLIT (unexhausted)
OORLICH
(miserable with cold etc.)
ORDINAR (ordinary)

The
minister's cat
is a PERJINK cat.

---

perjink &c [pərˈdʒɪŋk] *adj* **1** trim, neat, smart in appearance *la18-*. **2** prim, strait-laced *la18-*. **3** exact, precise, scrupulously careful, fussy *la18-*.

adv primly, fastidiously, in a precise and careful way *20-*.

n, in pl fussy details, niceties *e19*.   [only Sc; *per-* intensifier + prob onomat second element w infl f DINK, JINK¹ etc]

PAWKIE (lively, shrewd)
PERFERVID (ardent)
PERQUEER (expert)
PLACKLESS (penniless)
POOSHINOUS
(poisonous, horrible)

The
minister's cat is
a QUEESITIVE cat.

---

queesitive *adj* = inquisitive *la19-20, local Sh-Per*.

QUENT (quaint)
QUERTY
(vivacious, mischievous)
QUISQUOUS (doubtful)

The
minister's cat
is a RUNKLY cat.

---

runkle &c *vt* **1** wrinkle *la15-*. **2** crease, rumple, crush *18-, now Sh-nEC, WC, SW*. **3** gnarl, twist, distort, curl *18-, now local C*.
n a wrinkle, crease, ridged indentation *16-*.
runkly &c wrinkled *la18-, now NE nEC, WC, S*. [prob OScand *runkla* wrinkle; *cf* Dan *runken* wrinkled, Sw *rynka* wrinkle, Norw dial *rukka* a wrinkle; *cf* WRUNKLE]

RAM-STAM (rash, heedless)
RAUCLE (strong, rough)
REEZIE (tipsy)
ROARIE (drunk, loud)
RUMMLIN (boisterous)

The minister's cat is a SCUDDIE cat.

scuddie &c *adj* **1** naked, without clothes, or with one garment only *19-, now C, S*. **2** mean, scruffy, shabby-looking, in want or straitened circumstances *la19-e20*. **3** stingy, penurious; insufficient, too small *la19-, Bnf Abd*.

SAPSY (soppy)
SHOOGLIE (shaky, unsteady)
SLEEKIT (smooth, sly)
SONSIE (plump, attractive)
STOURIE (dusty)

The
minister's cat
is a THRAWN cat.

thrawn &c; throwin &c *la16,* **trawn &c**
la20-, Sh Ork Uls [θrɑn; *Abd also* 'θr(j)ɑvən] *adj*
1 twisted, crooked, distorted, misshapen *16-.*
2 *of the mouth, face* wry, twisted with pain, rage
etc, surly *16-.* **3** *of persons, animals, events* per-
verse, obstinate; intractable; cross, in a DOUR,
sullen mood *la15-.* **4** *of the weather* disagreea-
ble, inclement *la19-, now NE.*

TAPSIE-TEERIE (topsy-turvy)
TAUPIE (foolish)
TENTIE (careful)
TEUCHTER
(disparaging term for Highlander)
TOCHERLESS (without a dowry)

The minister's cat is an UNCO cat.

---

unco &c *18-;* **uncow &c** *16-e18,* **unca** *19-, now Abd,* **uncan &c** *19-, Sh,* **unkin &c** *la19-e20, Sh Ork* ['ʌŋkə; *Bwk Rox* 'ʌŋkɪ; *Edb also* 'ʌŋkɪ; *'ʌŋku] *adj* **1** (1) *of people, animals, things, places* (a) unknown, unfamiliar, strange *16-, now NE, C;* (b) so much altered as to be scarcely recognizable *19-, now Abd.* (2) *of countries or lands* foreign *19-, now Sh, only Sc; cf* UNCOUTH 2. **2** *also comparative* ∼**er** *la19-, superlative* ∼**est** *18-* unusual; odd, strange, peculiar *18-.* **3** remarkable, extraordinary, great, awful etc *18-, now NE Ags WC, only Sc: 'ye mak an unco sang about your taxes'.* **4** rude, uncouth, unseemly *18-e19, only Sc.* **5** reserved, shy, bashful *19-, now Sh, only Sc. adv* very, exceedingly, extremely *18-.*

UGSOME (repulsive)
UMBERSORROW (fit, robust)
UMQUHILE
(former, late, deceased)
UNBEKENT
(unobserved, unnoticed)
UNDEEMOUS (extraordinary)

The
minister's cat
is a VEEAND cat.

---

veeand &c [*ˈviən(d)] *adj* lacking common
sense; in one's dotage *19-e20, S.* [see VEED]

VAGRING (vagrant, wandering)
VAUDIE (vain, frisky)
VEECIOUS (vicious)
VOGIE (vain, light-hearted)

The minister's cat is a WULLCAT.

---

wild; wuld &c *e15, 19-e20,* **wile &c** *la16,
la19-, now Arg Wgt,* **will &c** *19-,* **wull &c** *19-*
[wəil(d), wɪl, wʌl; *Per also* wʌld] *adj* **1** = wild
la14-. **2** *of vocal sounds* loud and unrestrained
16-. **3** strong-tasting, rank *la19-, local Sh-nEC.*
4 nickname for the extreme Evangelical party
in the *Church of Scotland* (CHURCH) *la18-19.*
adv extremely, very *19-, local.*

wild cat &c *la15-,* **will cat &c** *la16-,* **wullcat
&c** *19-* = wild cat. **tummle** *etc* **the, one's** *or*
ower one's wullcat(s), wilkies &c tumble
head over heels, somersault *19-, chf WC;* cf *tum-*
mle or *turn the cat* (TUMMLE, TURN). **~ coal** poor
quality coal *19, WC.* **~fire 1** = wildfire *18-.*
2 summer lightning, lightning without thunder
la18-, now Ork-Per. **3** *mining* fire-damp *la19-,*
now Fif. **4** name of various wild flowers *19-,*
now Ags. **~ kail** the wild radish; the charlock
19-, SW. **~ parrot** an inferior kind of soft
coal *20-, Fif sEC, WC.* **~ rhubarb &c** the
common butterbur *la19-, Per-S.*

WABBIT (exhausted)
WAESOME (sorrowful)
WALLY (made of china)
WEE (small)
WERSH
(sickly, depressed, bitter-tasting)

The
minister's cat is
an XTRORNAR cat.

---

extraordinar &c;   **extrornar**   *18-19*
  ['ɛkstrə'ordnər,   ɛk'stror(d)nər,
  ɛkstər'ord(ə)nər] *adj* = extraordinary *la15-*.

XERCIT (experienced)
XTIRPIT (extirpated)
XTRANEARE (foreign)

The
minister's cat
is a YATTERY cat.

---

yatter &c *v* **1** *vi* nag, harp on querulously, scold *19-, local.* **2** chatter, ramble on, talk interminably *19-.* **3** *vti, of a person speaking incoherently or in a foreign language* gabble; *of an animal* yelp *19-.* **4** *vi, of teeth* rattle, chatter, *eg* from fear *20-, now Ags.*

n **1** (continual) scolding, grumbling *19-, now Ork Ags.* **2** continuous chatter, rambling and persistent talk *19-.* **3** the confused noise of many people talking loudly all together, clamour, unintelligible speech *19-, local Sh-Per.* **4** an incessant talker; a gossip *19-.*

~**in,** ~**y** fretful, querulous, scolding *19-, now Sh.* [only Sc; onomat; *cf* Eng *chatter,* NATTER, Norw dial *jaddre* jabber]

YALLOCHIE (yellowish)
YARE (ready, eager)
YAUPISH (clever, active)
YAWKIN (perplexed)

The
minister's cat
is a ZETLAND cat.

Zetland &c *16-* ['zɛtland; *'jɛtland; *see etymology*] = Shetland, used as the official name of the county until 1975, and as a peerage title. [ON *Hjaltland*, which developed (1) into *Sj- &c* in some Norw dials (> SHETLAND) and *Sh- &c* in Sc and Eng (*la13-*); (2) into *I-* or *Ih-* [j] in other Norw dials (*e13*), written in Sc as *Yh-* or *ʒ-* [j], the latter having the same form in Sc MSS and prints as *Z-* (see ʒ *letter*). The spelling-pronunciation [zɛt-] in place of the etymological [jɛt-] was established among the gentry and the professional classes by *e19*, and still survives alongside [ʃɛt-] (SHETLAND)]

ZEILLOUS (zealous)
ZULU (fishing-boat)